KARTS
AND
KARTING

KARTS AND KARTING

BY GEORGE S. FICHTER

FRANKLIN WATTS
NEW YORK/LONDON/
TORONTO/SYDNEY/1982
A FIRST BOOK

A GROLIER COMPANY

Cover photograph courtesy of:
International Kart Federation

Photographs courtesy of:
International Kart Federation: opposite title page and page 1,
pp. 3, 11, 21, 24, 26, 29, 32, 34, 35,
36, 39, 40, 43, 44, 46, 49, 50, 53;
United Press International: pp. 6, 14, 54.

THE AUTHOR AND EDITORS WOULD
LIKE TO THANK DOUG STOKES OF
THE INTERNATIONAL KART FEDERATION
FOR HIS VALUABLE TECHNICAL ASSISTANCE.

Library of Congress Cataloging in Publication Data

Fichter, George S.
Karts and karting.

(A First book)
Includes index.
Summary: Discusses the origin of the sport of
karting, type of engine and car used, racing events,
and the popularity this sport now enjoys.
1. Karting—Juvenile literature. 2. Karts
(Midget cars)—Juvenile literature. [1. Karting.
2. Karts (Midget cars)] I. Title.
GV1029.5.F52   796.7'6   *81-19681*
ISBN 0-531-04394-0   *AACR2*

CONTENTS

KARTS
AND
KARTING

CHAPTER ONE
THE WORLD OF KARTING

The high-pitched whine sounds like the scream of a powerful saw ready to slice into a log. Quickly it is joined by a second scream, then another and another. The whine becomes a roar—the sound of many motors, a tremendous buzzing like a swarm of angry bees.

A newcomer to Karting sees a dramatic spectacle. Strange little vehicles with tiny engines and bucket seats set in tubular bodyless frames dart around a track at breakneck speed. At first glance, a Kart looks as if it might achieve a top speed of 10 or maybe 15 miles per hour. But what Karts can do is truly astonishing. Hauling drivers that sometimes weigh 175 to 200 or more pounds (considerably more than the Karts themselves), the incredible little machines can go up to 125 miles per hour in a roadrace. In a sprint race, they glide around hairpin curves of a springwound course that allows a half-mile track to fit comfortably onto less than five acres. Here the Karts may accelerate to as much as 80 miles per hour on the straightaways. All this happens with the driver sitting only inches off the ground! It's a fantastic sight!

CHAPTER TWO
WHAT IS
A KART?

Forget all other kinds of miniature racers and "little cars," for Karts are not simply midget versions of larger cousins. Karts are unique. No other vehicles are like them. They are agile, responsive, and versatile. They can romp up and down hills. They can make quick turns, either right or left. They can also zip along straightaways.

Many of the larger race cars are much more restricted in what they can do. Some, for example, can make only left or right turns conforming to the kind of tracks laid out for them. Others cannot climb steep slopes. Still others are good only for fast speeds on short straightaways. Karts do not have these limitations. They can do everything any other race car can do.

The basic Kart consisted of a bucket seat set into a tubular and springless chassis, it moved on small wheels and was powered by a 2-cycle engine.

Pro sprint kart ready
for action—definitely
not a beginner's model.

Many variations of Karts have appeared over the years—and continue to appear—for there are really no design limits. A Kart enthusiast can, in fact, put together any sort of vehicle that suits a whim. Inventive Karters are always coming up with new designs to satisfy their creative urges. Sometimes a new production appeals greatly to other Karters, and a whole new trend is the result. After all, it was an experimental design that launched Karts in the beginning.

To enter official races, however, a Kart must meet particular specifications. These are established both for safety and to make fair matches in competition. They include the weight of the Kart, the driver, and the driver's gear. If a maverick vehicle with merit and appeal is demonstrated at the track, its worth may be recognized and copied by other Karters. Special new categories may then be added to permit these new designs to compete in sanctioned racing events.

While Karts were first powered only by a single, 2-cycle engine, some now are equipped with twin engines. Still others operate on 4-cycle engines. Both 2-cycle and 4-cycle engines are allowed to compete in separate classes. The Formula Kart Experimental category includes vehicles with transmissions (gearshifts) and enclosed bodies.

CHAPTER THREE
HOW KARTING BEGAN

No one is absolutely certain how Karts got their name. In 1957 the word "kart" first appeared in print in an automotive magazine where the little cars were called "go-karts." (The "go" part of the name has now been largely abandoned.) The magazine printed an article about the new little vehicles that had suddenly become popular in California.

Perhaps calling them "carts" seemed insulting considering what they could do. The "K" may have been chosen to give the word a special style.

The editors may have used the name jokingly, too, for many years ago there were baby buggies called Go Karts. It is possible the editors considered these little vehicles as "baby cars," parking lot playthings for children.

Before long, people began to understand that these vehicles do indeed GO—and at astonishing speeds. Karts became a permanent part of the sporting and recreational scene throughout the world.

SAYING
GOODBYE
TO HORSES

Motor-powered vehicles were born in France in the 1860s. Over the following years, inventors throughout the world worked at making them faster and more efficient. They attached motors to bicycles, tricycles, and every other kind of wheeled vehicle. Some of the inventions were ridiculous contraptions, but much was being learned about how to harness the driving power of the engine. By the 1890s, engine-powered vehicles were good enough to compete with horse-drawn carriages. The revolutionary explosion in manufacturing methods then occurred in America, and it brought about the era of the automobile.

Ever since, in fact, Americans have been "hooked" on wheels and motors. Automobiles started as fads that only the rich could afford. Owners made the most of showing off their machines. Then new production methods brought down costs. The car became not a fad but a necessity for getting people wherever they had to go in their daily lives. After World War II, it became common for a family to own two or more automobiles. And automobile driving came to be ranked by the government as the nation's biggest family recreation.

Over many years, young people constantly had before them the image of driving an automobile as the symbol of growing up and success. They wanted vehicles of their own. They

Actor Peter Sellers was actually a skilled racing driver. For this comedy role he had to pretend he didn't know how to drive. (Note the old-fashioned tires on this 1965 model.)

—7—

wanted the feeling of power and importance in controlling a machine, pushing it to its ultimate speed on straight stretches and piloting it skillfully around curves. And many young people and adults too enjoyed that unexplainable exhilaration that comes from racing. Racing vehicles—those used by professional racers—were large, complicated and much too expensive for the average nonprofessional to afford.

Parents and young people with know-how began to rig up vehicles that answered these desires for "something to drive." A workable gasoline engine from a lawn mower or an outboard motor supplied the necessary power. This might be attached to a frame made of two-by-fours. Wheels often came from an old wagon. Bicycle sprockets and chains were used to transfer the engine's power to the wheels. A steering wheel connected to the front wheels completed the vehicle and made it ready to go.

Many enterprising amateurs took a few more steps. They made a boxlike hood and gave their creation a fancy paint job. Some of these backyard cars were ugly ducklings at best, while others were surprisingly handsome. But the important point was that they had engines, made noises, and could be driven just like big cars.

These "little cars" were driven down alleys, on sidewalks, through parking lots—everywhere but into the main stream of traffic with the big cars. Most performed at a rocketing five miles per hour or a little more. But wherever they went and at whatever speed, they caused a sensation. The proud owners were the envy of the neighborhood.

From coast to coast, this kind of story was repeated. Most of the vehicles were similar, though there was no formal pattern. Parents and kids simply put together what was practical with available materials and limited engineering skill. Some were a bit faster or prettier than others, but there were very few revolutionary designs.

THE FIRST
REAL KART

Then came Art Ingles. A professional race-car designer for a California manufacturer, Art had engineered many of the racing cars used in the Indy 500. He knew how to make fast cars in big dimensions, but suddenly he felt the desire to make a "little car." Using his engineering experience, Art put together his own version of a parking-lot vehicle. Although he did not set out to do so, it was really Art Ingles who spawned the explosive sport of Karting. It happened that he made his "little car" at precisely the time when the public was ready to receive it.

Art Ingles used a lawn mower motor and a frame of metal tubing. Compared to Karts today, his first creation sat rather high off the ground—four inches, in fact. It had an upright seat, and there was no "front porch" for the driver's legs as there is in Karts today. When Art sat in his "little car," his knees stuck up almost as high as his head. But Art's car was definitely a pioneering phenomenon. He made his first run with the little vehicle in the parking lot of the Rose Bowl in Pasadena, California, and amazed even himself by zipping along at about 30 miles per hour.

Everyone who saw Art Ingles' "little car" was fascinated. People wanted to know where he got it and how they could get one. Among those who watched the early performances of the little vehicle was Duffy Livingstone. He was one of Art's close friends and was also deeply involved in racing. Duffy quickly made a twin of Art's little vehicle. Then together they made

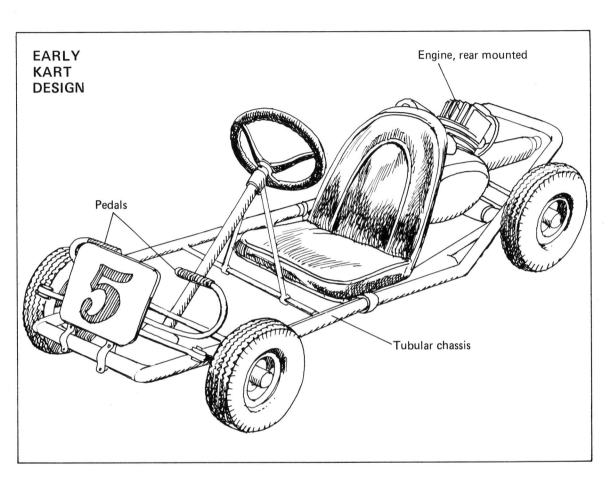

EARLY KART DESIGN

Engine, rear mounted

Pedals

5

Tubular chassis

This is what the early "little cars" looked like. (Note that the engine was mounted in back.)

A modern sprint racer. This one has two side-mounted engines. The wide, slick tires are for driving on paved tracks.

more. Soon they had about a dozen in operation. Naturally they began staging informal contests to see which car was fastest and who had the best driving skill. Pure fun was the major objective of these early Kart races and is still the principal focus of Karting today. The cost was so small that almost no one was excluded from having a try. And from the very beginning, enthusiasts of all ages took to modifying their little cars to improve performance and handling.

Kart racing has since become a worldwide sport. It offers all the thrills and excitement of big car races.

CHAPTER FOUR FUN KARTING

Challenging other Kart owners in races is unquestionably one of the big reasons Karting is so popular today, but the joy of Karting is not confined to racing. Many people get great pleasure from their Karts without racing.

But where can Karts be driven?

Karts may not be driven legally on streets and highways. They are too small and low to be clearly visible in traffic. Hence they are a hazard both to the Karters and to the drivers of conventional vehicles. A Kart could not, in fact, even display a license plate at a normal height. Sometimes Karting clubs can have streets or roads officially blocked off for special events, but between these times, where can they go?

Vacant parking lots or similar large areas of asphalt or concrete are excellent places when permission is granted for their use. If you own a Kart, be sure to check before you and your Karting friends choose such a place to run your vehicles. Property owners have to consider their liability in case of accidents, not only to the Karters but also to the spectators—for

Where can you drive a Kart? Around the castle, of course. England's Prince Charles at age twenty driving his younger brother Edward around the castle grounds.

people naturally show up to watch when they hear the whine of Kart engines.

Karters often form local clubs for this reason. A group may be able to work out an arrangement where an individual could not. And clubs can provide the necessary insurance. Kart dealers are often helpful in organizing clubs. They know Karts and Karting and they also hope that club members will buy their products.

Across the country, hundreds of tracks have been built in recent years although only a few have been built just for Karts. Most serve several needs.

A good half-mile track with plenty of twists and turns to give a Karter a test of driving skill can fit comfortably into five acres or less. Some tracks of this kind are privately owned and are near Kart shops. The shop owners often make their tracks available at night or other times for private runs and for sanctioned races.

At many of these tracks Karts can be rented. The engines of rental cars are controlled by governors, devices that hold down their speed.

Compared to the well-tuned, high-performance vehicles driven by racers, rental cars are definitely low-key. They generally go no faster than 20 miles per hour, and usually less. But that is fast enough for first-time and inexperienced drivers. For some, rental cars are enough and provide almost all of the thrills without the possible risks involved in competitive events. For others, rental cars are only a start. They look forward to entering in competitive events with their own vehicles.

At Karting tracks, young drivers learn good driving habits and the importance of driving rules and regulations. Good, safe driving becomes automatic. This is one of the big pluses for

Karting. The fundamentals of driving are learned in a controlled and highly organized Karting situation rather than out on the highway. At the same time, Karting supplies qualified drivers with a regulated outlet for whatever it is in some people that makes them want to go fast and to race.

CHAPTER
FIVE
WHAT POWERS
A KART?

Power for the conventional Kart comes from a 2-cycle internal combustion engine of the same sort that drives lawn mowers, power saws, hedge trimmers, and outboards. They are not as economical in their use of fuel as are larger, more complicated engines, but compared in size, they deliver much more power. Now engines specially designed to supply power for Karts are available.

Internal combustion describes the basic process by which the engines operate. It means that the explosive burning of the fuel takes place inside the engine. In nearly all engines of this type, the hot gases from the burned fuel are converted to driving energy by a piston that moves up and down in an enclosed cylinder. The first successful internal combustion engine was invented in the 1870s by Nikolaus Otto. Though it was primitive and inefficient compared to present-day engines, the Otto cycle engine is the ancestor of all of the internal combustion engines now in use. The Otto engine got only one power stroke from every two turns of the engine's crankshaft, or four strokes of the piston. In 2-cycle engines, as used in Karts, a

TWO-STROKE ENGINE CYCLE

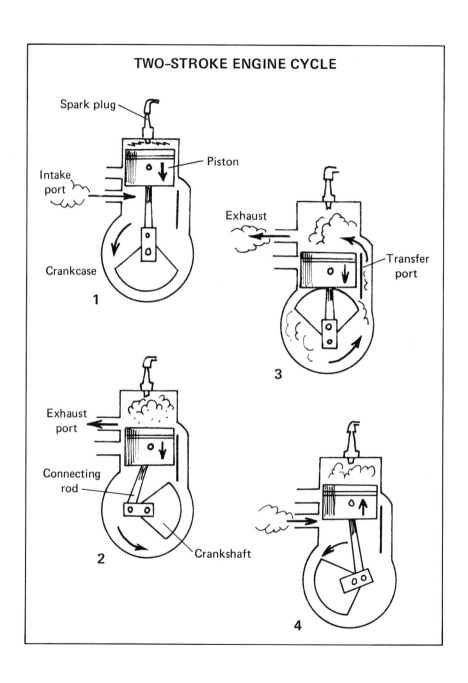

power stroke is obtained from a single rotation of the crank-shaft, or two strokes of the piston.

Yet the two-stroke or 2-cycle engine's operation is really very simple. This is indeed one of its charms. The engines are so easily understood that even beginners can tinker with them to correct problems or to improve on their performance. Surprisingly, some people who know and understand more complicated engines may have difficulty with these engines because of their simplicity. This makes it easy for a beginner to start out even with those who might at first seem to be more knowledgeable.

Like all other internal combustion engines, the two-stroke engine operates as a result of explosions in the cylinders in rapid succession. To start the engine, the crankshaft is rotated. This may be done by pulling a cord or by power supplied from a battery. In most engines, the fuel is gasoline mixed with oil for lubrication, generally in 20:1 ratio. It may also be a mixture of alcohol and oil.

The fuel is mixed with air in the carburetor before going into the cylinder. The spark plug ignites the fuel to start the power stroke which drives the piston down (see diagram, page 18). At the same time, the fuel-and-air mixture from the carburetor is drawn through the intake port into the crank-case (Fig. 1). As the piston goes down, the intake port is closed off and the exhaust port is open, allowing the burned gases to exit (Fig. 2). The mixture of fuel and air in the crank-case moves up into the cylinder through the transfer port (Fig. 3). During the compression stroke the exhaust port is closed and the fuel-air mixture is compressed to prepare for the next spark from the spark plug (Fig. 4). Each explosive burning also generates large amounts of heat. Big fins on the engine help to radiate this heat away and keep the engine as cool as possible.

The internal firing continues rapidly, the piston moving up and down. Lubrication for the engine's moving parts comes from the oil that is mixed with the gasoline. Engines used in racing vehicles may operate at 8,000 to 16,000 revolutions per minute. Racers sometimes regulate their engines while they are in motion. This is done by adjusting the critical fuel and air mixtures by a hand screw located on the carburetor. Experienced drivers get their mixtures just right by listening to their engines, though many of the better and more sophisticated engines have gauges to measure the tremperature and the engine's revolutions per minute. A really good ear tells the experienced Karter when the engine is operating at its peak power and best performance for the particular demands being made on it. An engine with too much fuel compared to oxygen —too rich a mixture—does not have peak power. To run more strongly the amount of fuel must be reduced. But if there is too much air compared to fuel, the engine may stop running, or "konk out."

Racers "rebuild" their engines about every six hours of racing time to replace parts that are worn or damaged by the intense heat or by the friction of the fast movement. This assures the racer that his engine is always in top operating condition.

In the beginning, all of the engines used for Karts were manufactured exclusively in the United States where Karting was born. Art Ingles, for example, used a West Bend engine that had been manufactured originally to run a lawn mower. There was an immediate clamor for those engines, which had temporarily been discontinued, but soon others entered the field. Many motors now are built especially to accommodate the particular and demanding needs of Karts.

CRANKSHAFT

PISTON

*The two halves of the motor, shown,
fit like a sandwich on either
end of the crankshaft. The cylinder
will fit on the four long bolts.*

West Bend engines were joined by engines made by McCulloch, Clinton, Homelite, Briggs-Stratton, Margay, and others. Some of these engines, modified especially for Karts, are still being produced. But today the engine field is dominated by foreign products—the Yamaha from Japan, the Parilla from Italy, the T.K.M. from England, and others. The prices for foreign engines are higher than for American-made motors, but for racing, they give a performance that makes the difference worth it to the drivers.

CHAPTER SIX SPRINT RACES

From its parking-lot beginnings, Karting quickly became a full-fledged racing sport. The earliest of the several kinds of Kart racing is the sprint race. Sprint races are high-speed events for short distances on hard-surfaced (asphalt) tracks that are up to three-fourths of a mile long. The tracks have numerous twists and turns. Rarely are the straightaways longer than 300 feet, but even at these short distances, the rocketing little cars someimes attain speeds of 60 to 80 miles per hour.

At the track, each entrant is assigned an off-track "pit," an area where the driver and crew can do necessary work on the vehicle before a race starts. These areas are alongside the track but well out of the way of the Karts that are running. Drivers can pull their cars into the pit area to make emergency repairs. The engines must be stopped after the Kart crosses a designated entrance line to the pit area. They are then pushed to their assigned pit. When they are ready to leave, the Kart must be pushed to the entry line before the motor is started. Each driver is allowed only two helpers in the pit.

Sprint races are run in three separate "heats," each of which is ten laps around the track. The winner of the race is the driver who scores the most combined points for all three heats.

Starting positions at the beginning of the race are determined by pre-race time trials in which a driver races only against the clock. The winners of the first heat then get front starting positions in the second heat, and winners of the second heat become first starters in the third heat. In these races it is an obvious advantage to be a first runner in each performance on the track, especially in the time trials.

Sprint Karts look much like the original Karts. The driver sits upright or with only a slight backward tilt. But unlike the first Karts, the new versions have an ample "front porch" so that even long-legged drivers can stretch out their legs comfortably. Also, the engines are mounted at the side rather than behind the seat, and the fuel tank is in front—mounted under the steering wheel. The form-fitting bucket seats, made of fiberglass, are padded, covered with a tough leatherlike plastic, and are comfortable. The aircraft-tubing chassis is strong but lightweight. It has enough "give" so that the responsive vehicles can be driven into curves with a minimum of braking. To keep the Kart's weight at a minimum, lightweight materials such as aluminum, fiberglass, and plastic are used wherever possible. In most Karts the steering wheel, seats, pedals, and other parts are movable within limits so they can be adjusted to a particular driver's needs for best driving.

The first Karts wore thin treaded tires much like those you see on lawn mowers and small garden tractors today. Most fun Karts still have treaded tires. But the tires on sprint Karts are slick, without treads, and they are two or three times wider than the familiar treaded tires. Made especially for Karts, they stick to the asphalt track better than do those with treads.

*Tight competition in the I.K.F. Grandnationals
at MacArthur Park in Lawton, Oklahoma.*

Power is transmitted to the rear wheels by an oil clutch on the engine's crankshaft. The drive is through a chain that connects a sprocket on the engine to a sprocket on the rear wheel.

There are numerous sprint tracks all over the United States. Sprint events are also staged in other countries. The World Championships, in fact, are held in Europe, and in this event there are entrants from countries throughout the world.

Sprint-race events are in five major divisions: Junior Rookie (ages 7-9), Junior (ages 9-15), Novice (ages 16 and over), Amateur (ages 16 and over), and Expert (ages 16 and over). Many of the drivers in the Expert class today actually started in the Junior class. The classes are divided first according to the driver's age, but the size and type of the Kart as well as the minimum weight of the Kart and driver are also important factors.

According to International Kart Federation specifications, the minimum Kart weight for a single-engine entry in a sprint race is 85 pounds. The minimum for a dual-engine entry is 105 pounds .The wheelbase, measured from the center of the front and rear wheel axles, is 50 inches maximum and 40 inches minimum. The total length of the Kart from front to rear cannot be more than 72 inches, and the maximum height of the vehicle cannot be more than 26 inches. The minimum width from the center line of the right front tire to the center line of the left front tire is 28 inches. The maximum allowable tire diameter is 19.5 inches; the minimum is 9 inches. Only pneumatic tires are allowed. No Kart may have more than four wheels.

The Kart may not have a body, and the steel tubes used for the chassis must be no less than an inch in diameter and have walls at least 0.08 of an inch thick. The tubing must be made of steel or of a material of equal strength. Seat belts are not allowed. Wheels must be secured to the axle with safety wire or cotter keys.

The compartment for the driver must have side rails, and the driver must be contained completely inside the specified length and width of the chassis. Every vehicle must have approved bumpers, and they must be within the vehicle's maximum allowable length. The driver's feet may not project beyond the front bumper.

Other International Kart Federation specifications cover the fuel system, the amount of ballast allowed (and this must be bolted to the frame), the type and securing of the steering mechanism, types of clutches and brakes, and other factors. These specifications are reviewed regularly and may be added to or altered by the governing officials of the organization. Any changes or variations are communicated immediately to member organizations that run sanctioned races.

Before each event, every Kart must be weighed in and pass a rigorous safety inspection by the race officials. The inspection covers the Kart's basic design, all of its parts and their operation, and also the Kart's appearance. The Karts must also be inspected in an impounding area after a race to make certain they still conform to the requirements and that no alterations were made while the race was in progress. Winners are not announced until this inspection is completed, and the inspections are careful and thorough.

As a result of these strict regulations, Kart races have an excellent safety record, unsurpassed in motor vehicle competitions. Precautions are taken to keep them that way. Emer-

Before the race: waiting for the command: "Start your engines!"

gency equipment—an ambulance and trained medics—must be available at all events. A driver's helmet must show clearly his or her full name, blood type, Rh factor, and any particular allergies or other information that might be important in the event medical attention is needed.

The drivers themselves must conform to a set of rigid safety regulations. First of all, their general appearance must be approved by the race officials. Helmets and goggles or face shields are required, as are heavy racing jackets, gloves, and full-length trousers. A driver will be disqualified from a race because of an unsafe or faulty Kart or because of reckless driving or a poor attitude during a race.

FLAGS

After a race is started, flags are the only way officials can communicate with the drivers. The drivers have to demonstrate their understanding of these waved signals.

A green flag is displayed when a race is started. As long as the green flag continues to be shown, racers know that the track is clear for continued racing.

A yellow flag means caution. Drivers have to slow down and passing is not allowed. Drivers must be prepared to stop immediately if necessary. They can proceed at full speed only after the green flag appears again.

A red flag commands drivers to stop safely, but at once. It signifies that the track has become unsafe. Drivers must go immediately to an impounding area. While they wait in this area, they are not permitted to work on their vehicles.

A blue flag indicates that a faster racer is trying to pass, and the slower racer must allow room for this to happen.

A white flag, used in sprint races, tells racers they have only one more lap to go in the race.

A white flag with a red cross in its center signals drivers to slow down and not to pass because an emergency vehicle is on the track.

Black flags are used to signal particular drivers. A waved black flag tells a driver to continue one more lap at a slower speed and then stop by the racing official who is giving the signal. The Kart may have a mechanical problem such as a fuel- or oil-leak; or the pit crew may be violating some regulation, in which case the driver must return to the pit and instruct the crew to observe regulations.

A rolled black flag warns the driver that his or her driving technique borders on disqualification. If the driver continues to drive in the same manner, the car will be black-flagged and possibly disqualified.

A checkered flag signals the end of the race. When this flag is shown, the drivers are expected to continue around the track one more time at reduced speed and then to stop in the impounding area for their post-race inspection.

The race is over!

In most races, small entrance fees are charged to cover the expenses of the race, and the winners get trophies, not money. There are professional races, however, in which the winners drive for cash awards. The entry fees in these special races are high, and the winners may get sums in the thousands of dollars.

Manufacturers contribute substantially to the professional races, for these events give them a chance to showcase the performance and value of their products. Because of the manufacturers' participation, professional races get attention from television, radio, newspapers, and magazines. Ads featuring specific Karts or parts used by the winners may give the events national attention for months after they were held, and then the ads begin billing the next events. The winners in these

races become important personalities in the sports world, and their names are well known.

Lake Speed, Mark Dismore, Lynn Haddock, Terry Traeder —these are among the Kart-racing stars of professional races known not only in the United States but around the world. Lake Speed won the World Championship in France in 1978, the first American to do so. While Karting did start in the United States, the top competitors in the professional races had always been from other countries until Lake Speed's victory. But the picture is now changing. More Americans are geared up for wins.

The professional racers have their own organization—the Professional Kart Association (PKA). A driver must be well into Karting before he or she is ready for membership in this group.

Lake Speed
(1978 World Karting
Champion) waits his turn
for pro qualifying at
Jacksonville, Florida.

Bruce Jenner, 1976 Decathlon
Champion, is a Karter. Here he is
driving a dual-motored sprint kart.
National Champion Joe Giroski
holding the "Duffy" trophy (right).

CHAPTER SEVEN
DIRT OR SPEEDWAY RACES

Dirt or speedway races are very similar to sprint races. They are run on tracks that are ordinarily used for motorcycle and stock car races. Most of these tracks are ovals, but a few are irregular, giving Karters an opportunity to demonstrate their vehicles' versatility. Though they vary in length, the typical Karting speedway track is a quarter of a mile long or less. It has a surface of packed dirt or clay rather than asphalt.

The Karts used in dirt races are essentially the same as those used in sprint races, but there are a few modifications. Their tires are wider and have treads cut in them to give better traction in the dirt. Because of the dust, the engines are equipped with very efficient air filters to prevent the engines from choking. The Karts also have a front fairing, which is a fiberglass panel that fits over the steering wheel. It serves as a protective shield against stones or other debris thrown up from the track by the speeding racers.

Dirt racing has grown rapidly in popularity in the United States because of the prevalence of tracks used for other events. Kart races now contribute to keeping the tracks in use, and they give spectators a new and exciting style of racing to watch. Because of the "loose" dirt surface, speedway Karts can "get sideways" in spectacular controlled skids, and because of the clouds of dust, they are exciting to watch and a challenge to the drivers. Both the drivers and their Karts generally come out of these races caked with mud.

Dirt races are typically run in three heats. The first two have ten laps each, and the final heat has 20 laps. In the lineup for the second heat, the faster Karts are lined up behind the slower ones to make for equal competition. In the final heat, racers are positioned by their accumulated points in the first two heats. The winners of the race are determined by their total points in all three heats. It is possible, though not likely, to finish poorly in the first two heats and still win the overall race.

ICE RACING

In the past, most Karts had to be "mothballed" in winter except in the South and West. Karters tinkered with engines and did other work on their vehicles in basements and garages while they waited for the winds of spring.

But ice racing is now keeping many Karters in action in Wisconsin, Minnesota, Michigan, and other iced-in areas. The same basic rules and regulations apply in ice races, but the

Lee Hatch (age fourteen) is International Kart Federation's three-time national Jr. Speedway champ. In this picture his Kart is shown on slicks for sprint racing.

Karts wear different tires. Most are studded to give them a more secure grip on the ice. Some Karters put chains on their tires. They wrap the chain tightly on the tire while it is not fully inflated and then inflate the tire fully to pull the chain even tighter. Karters say their chain-clad vehicles run as though on rails. Most important, they are more easily controlled, and they can be controlled with less skidding and sliding.

It is not possible for Karts to go as fast on ice as they do on conventional tracks. But the thrills for both the participants and the spectators are magnified.

Karting on snow and ice
in Helsinki, Finland.

CHAPTER EIGHT ENDURO RACES

Enduro or roadraces give Karters an opportunity to demonstrate their vehicles' superlative speeds and endurance over long distances. For enduro races, Karts carry more fuel—usually in two tanks, one mounted on each side. Most of the races last for at least an hour. The Karts are started side by side—about two feet between each. There are no warm-up laps, but the engines can be started a minute before the race to get them ready.

Drivers in enduro races drive in a "laid back" or recumbent position. This is not only more comfortable but also makes the vehicle and driver more streamlined for achieving speeds of 100 miles per hour or greater.

Enduro races are held on big tracks, such as at Daytona (Florida), Watkins Glen (New York), and Riverside (California). These are the tracks used by the professionals who drive the big race cars. The tracks vary in length from two to over four miles. As many as 500 to 600 Karters participate in these events. Fifty or more Karts may be on the track at the same time. The Kart finishing the most laps in the specified time for the race (usually one hour) is declared the winner.

In many roadracing Karts, the rear wheels are driven by a special rubber drive belt rather than a chain. Commonly the belt is connected to the axle or to the engine by a centrifugal axle clutch. This type of clutch requires no oil, which makes it clean in operation, but the proper adjustment is extremely delicate. Roadracing Karts with six-speed transmissions and with engines twice the size of those used on sprint Karts are becoming more common. Many are powered with motorcycle engines of 270 cubic centimeters.

Roadracing Karts differ from sprint Karts also in their exhaust systems. The adjustable "slippy" exhaust pipe is connected by a cable to the steering wheel, and the driver may change the length of the pipe while the Kart is in motion. On corners or in curves, these engines perform better with a "short" pipe. On straightaways, more power is obtained with a "long" pipe.

Roadracing Karts are obviously much more expensive than are the simpler and smaller fun Karts and sprint racers. They are more difficult to maintain, too. Roadracing is not how most people get started in Karting, but for many people it is the eventual goal. The most elaborate Karts are those in the Formula Kart Experimental category. FKEs have enclosed bodies and do indeed look like miniature versions of big racing automobiles.

The International Kart Federation's specifications for roadracers require a minimum weight of 95 pounds for single-en-

Driver 21 acknowledges a flag waved by the starters, telling him there is one more lap to go.

gined vehicles or 115 pounds for dual engines. The maximum allowable wheelbase is 50 inches from the axle centers of the wheels; the minimum is 40 inches. The maximum allowable Kart length is 80 inches. (Dual-motored machines may use aerodynamic wings and noses, and have no overall restriction on length.) The minimum width, measured from the center of a tire on one side to the center of a tire on the other side, is 40 inches. And the maximum allowable height is 26 inches. The tires on roadracing Karts are "slicks," like those on sprint racers.

Two superkarts racing in the rain. Note the laid-back position of the drivers.

CHAPTER
NINE
THE APPEAL
OF KARTING

Karts began as sports vehicles for young people, and young people are still very much a part of Karting. The vast majority of Karts are owned and operated by drivers in their early teens and younger. But most top Karting drivers—the racers—are over the age of 20. (And many of the best are girls and young women.) Nearly all of these expert drivers started Karting when they were teenagers or younger.

Challenging other Kart owners in races is one of the reasons why Karting is so popular, but people enjoy Karting for many other reasons as well. For many Karters the fun comes from simply piloting these maneuverable and spirited little vehicles around a track. Others take pleasure in the purr of a well-tuned motor. They enjoy tinkering with the engine or altering the design of the vehicle to get the greatest power and performance. Karting gives others a feeling of independence.

While some drivers never race, racing is probably the most widespread aspect of the sport. And it is in racing that new

**Tension at post-race technical inspection.
You've won on the track, but is your motor all right?**

designs for Kart engines, bodyless chassis, and other parts are developed and tested. (In just the same way, big car racing has made a great contribution to our everyday automobiles.) Those who do not race benefit from the inventive engineering that goes into getting the most from engines used in the racing events.

Kart racers have a great desire to compete and a thorough knowledge of the Karts themselves and how they operate. Racing is more expensive than simple pleasure Karting, however. Racers also need money to buy equipment and to travel to and from the tracks. (Most Karters, for example, use specially built trailers or vans for hauling their vehicles and equipment.)

If your goal is racing, then you might want to get in touch with one or both of the organizations listed in the back of this book. They can be helpful in getting started in the right direction. A first timer can best learn the fundamentals of Kart design and handling by getting a used machine in good condition.

Perhaps your main interest is in operating a Kart of your own design. If you have learned the basics well, be persistent. You may have an idea that will revolutionize Karting. Karters are always on the lookout for innovations.

If you live in a beach area, for example, you might design a Kart that can manage the sand. It would, of course, be higher than the conventional Kart, but it might open up many miles of pleasure driving. Or if you live where there is a lot of open country, you might design a special Kart for off-road or cross-country terrain.

Junior drivers must get permission, of course, whether the focus is racing or driving for fun. As a result sometimes a whole family becomes involved in Karting.

CHAPTER
TEN
THE KART
EXPLOSION

When Art Ingles made his historic drive in 1956 around the Rose Bowl parking lot, only a few dozen Karts existed. After 1957 they multiplied like rabbits. Suddenly there were Karts everywhere. Almost overnight Karting became popular everywhere in the world. Eager buyers clamored for Kart kits, engines, tires, and other parts. Within less than five years there were more than 600 manufacturers of Karts and their parts. It was far too many.

There are always excesses when something new comes on the scene and people jump into the action without experience. Many of the new enterprises were "shoestring" operations that collapsed quickly when up against strong competitors. Finally the Karting industry stabilized. Now a dozen or so top manufacturers exist, supported by several dozen more that supply parts and materials.

While the number of industries and supplies stabilized, the number of Kart shops increased. Nearly all are now owned and operated by people who are much involved with Karts and Karting themselves. For this reason, these are places where

A father sees to wiping his son's "windshield."

**A happy winner is hoisted
along with his vehicle at the
world championships in Italy.**

beginners can find out about Karts and get reliable advice about motors, the best kinds of chassis, and other Karting information.

If you are a beginner, you might go first of all to a Kart shop for information. Then visit a track and check your information by talking to some of the experienced drivers. It is a good idea to make several trips to one or more tracks to see who is driving what kind of equipment. Then ask the drivers why they made their particular choices. Most drivers are understanding and willing to help. They probably recall when they were just beginning and had similar questions.

KARTING
ORGANIZATIONS

Karting is now represented by two major organizations. One is the International Kart Federation (IKF), which has its headquarters in California. The other is the World Karting Association (WKA), with headquarters in Ohio. They are listed in the back of this book along with other Karting information.

The two groups are very similar in function. IKF sanctions races mainly west of the Mississippi, and WKA puts on events east of the Mississippi. But these areas of activity overlap more and more often. For example, the IKF's 1981 Grandnational Roadracing Championships were held at Blackhawk Farms, near Beloit, Wisconsin. The two organizations established the rules and regulations that govern all of the official Karting events. They supply information about new products, lists of tracks, information about insurance to cover participation in a sanctioned event, and information about local Karting clubs. Their members receive a monthly magazine that covers Karting events and subjects of general interest to enthusiasts.

KARTING WORDS

Axle clutch: A clutch located on the axle rather than on the motor shaft. (The axle clutch is popular in roadracing.)

Bicycle: To go up on two wheels in a turn. (Bicycling is caused by too much speed on very "sticky" tires.)

Dirt machine: A speedway Kart. (Speedway races are run on dirt tracks.)

Drafting: Staying just behind a lead car to take advantage of the "hole in the air" created by the lead car.

Duffy: The highest award in Karting, given to the Karting Grandnational champion in each class, named for Duffy Livingstone, a Karting pioneer.

Front porch: That part of a Kart that extends in front of the front axle.

Laydown: An old name for the enduro or roadracing Karts in which the driver sits in a laid back position.

Rocket: The driver of a very fast machine.

Shoe: The driver of a racing machine. (The driver stomps the gas pedal, hence "shoe.")

Sidewinder: a side-mounted engine. The term came into use when engines began to be mounted alongside the driver rather than in the rear.

Situp: Standard Kart driving position; the opposite of "laydown."

Skins: Tires (also called "meat," "rubber," "Do-nuts," and "roundies").

Slippy pipe: Exhaust system than can be adjusted during the race for more power.

Slipstreaming: See "drafting."

Stagger: To use tires of different circumference on the rear axle for different handling characteristics.

Sticky tires: Modern technology has allowed the development of racing tires that are literally sticky to the touch.

Tach: A device that counts motor revolutions (RPM) and displays the motor speed on a gauge for the driver to check.

Teching: Inspection of the Kart before a race to see that it conforms to safety rules; also inspection after a race to check "legality" of motor size, fuel type, weight, etc.

Temp Gauge: A temperature gauge attached to the steering wheel that tells how hot the motor is.

Zip: To pass another competitor rapidly, as "He really zipped old Jim!"

MORE INFORMATION

KARTING ORGANIZATIONS

International Kart Federation (IKF)
416 South Grand Avenue
Covina, California 91724

Professional Kart Association (PKA)
P.O. Box 105
Edison, California 93220

World Karting Organization (WKA)
P.O. Box 2548
North Canton, Ohio 44720

KARTING MAGAZINES

WORLD KARTING
P.O. Box 2548
North Canton, Ohio 44720

KARTER NEWS
416 South Grand Avenue
Covina, California 91724

KARTING
Karting Bookshop
Bank House
Summerhill, Chislehurst
Kent, England

KART-TECH
P.O. Box 488
Star, North Carolina 27356

KART MANUFACTURERS AND SUPPLIERS

Here are some of the major manufacturers
of Karts and Kart supplies.
The list will supply your needs
if there are no Kart shops near you
or if you prefer to "do it yourself."

Azusa Engineering
1542 Industrial Park Street
Covina, California 91722

Bell Helmets
2850 East 29th Street
Long Beach, California 90806

Blackhawk Karts
Route 2, Box 194
Brodhead, Wisconsin 53520

Bridgestone Tire Company
2160 West 190th Street
Torrance, California 90504

Bronco
P.O. Box 260
Cornwell Heights, Pennsylvania 19020

Carlisle Tire and Rubber Company
P.O. Box 99
Carlisle, Pennsylvania 17013

Cassella Engineering
4A Bethpage Road
Copiague, New York 11726

Haddock Ltd.
2511 McCallie Avenue
Chattanooga, Tennessee 37404

Hartman Engineering
3731 Oark Place
Montrose, California 91020

Hornet Manufacturing
1112 Columbus Avenue
Waco, Texas 76701

Horstman Manufacturing Company, Inc.
730 East Huntington Drive
Monrovia, California 91016

K & P Manufacturing
330 South Irwindale Avenue
Azusa, California 91702

Margay Products
3185 South Kingshighway
St. Louis, Missouri 63139

McCulloch
6101 West Century Boulevard
Los Angeles, California 90045

Nelson Manufacturing
745 McGlincey Lane
Campbell, California 95008

Eobson, Incorporated
436 North Cook Street
Bennettsville, South Carolina 29512

Speed-Karts
P.O. Box 9285
Jackson, Mississippi 39206

Yamaha
P.O. Box 6620
Buena Park, California 90622

INDEX